AuthorHouse™
1663 Liberty Drive
Bloomington, IN 47403
www.authorhouse.com
Phone: 833-262-8899

Published by AuthorHouse 01/23/2023

ISBN: 978-1-7283-7775-9 (sc)
ISBN: 978-1-7283-7774-2 (e)

brary of Congress Control Number: 2023901019

Print information available on the last page.

epicted in stock imagery provided by Getty Images are models,
ch images are being used for illustrative purposes only.
Certain stock imagery © Getty Images.

This book is printed on acid-free paper.

The
cons
of Fre

A Monograph on the

C A R L O S

authorHO

CONTENTS

DEDICATION

I dedicate this book to my sister Daisy Miller who at the time of the writing of this book 2017, is in a federal prison, doing time for a crime she did not commit. Sentenced to do years in prison for a crime that was considered a "conspiracy to commit fraud." "Conspiracy:" a word that keeps coming up and is being used for the explicit purpose of putting someone in a warehouse because it suits the political purpose of a few prosecutors and judges. The lies that were put forth, the fabrication of so called evidence, and the use of false witnesses is a trend that has taken over our courts; our system is failed, and our society slowly sinks into obscurity.

SERAFIN

Carlos De Jesus Verdugo.

THE TEMPLE I SHALL BUILD

I wish to build a house,

A temple if I could,

And if my hand allows,

On the place wherein I stood.

I searched for lumber, stone, and silt.

The more I search,

The more I'd have built,

For my house, my temple, my church.

I met a man at the grange,

His hands and feet full of thorns.

His face was old, yet not strange.

His head, a crown of fire adorns.

I asked if he could spare a brick or two.

The shape of the stone could be large or small.

It mattered not to me because I knew,

Behind him stood a mountain with them all.

However it be or may cost,

Odd and even, brittle and rent,

For nothing gained is nothing lost,

When all we've lost is time we've spent.

All of the stones that I've found,

Lay in silence without man

Shaping the stones with the sound

Of tools splitting the hard sand.

Nothing said is nothing heard,

Yet we can still hear the noise

Of the house in which we were;

That same house, time now destroys.

The stone, the tools, and the wood

Are all those that came before.

The corner stone that we would

Become is something much more.

None will finish his temple

'Fore others' have been erected.

Be he hurried and careful,

No sooner will it be collected.

All of the stones shall be used

And shall be that last vestige,

We could not have then refused,

For these stones are in our image.

And we are that very same

Rubble of wood, tools, and stone

That we now look at and claim

Is our own flesh, blood, and bone.

PREFACE

The following essay was due to the inspiration of a seven-year discussion with a very good friend and brother, Brother Gerald E. Connally, whose background is quite extensive and his knowledge of FM∴ and ancient history is well-versed. Our seven-year-long discussion has taken us on a journey to the understanding of the psychological state of mind of our present society. Whether or not this psychological state of mind of our current society is meaningful, it has its roots in the past. Our fraternity was established for a purpose, and that purpose along with a learning journey which myself and Gerald E. Connally have taken leads us to believe that we are still on a quest. A wise man once said, "there is but one truth in this world, and that is that there is no truth in it." Our quest is for the truth, and we believe that it does exist; it simply has been hidden by nature, who reveals herself every now and then as she did with Moses in the desert. Today, we too venture into that desert and seek her truth.

I have chosen to write largely in the first person singular because life is a journey, Freemasonry is that journey for those who choose it. It is a uniquely individual journey, but one our brothers are also taking. Each of us walks it for himself, knowing that those about him are his brothers and stand willing to help, as must he.

INTRODUCTION

As history repeats itself time and again, the "isms" run their course and self-destruct. The real battle is and always has been Oligarchs versus Entrenched Bureaucrats. And when the inevitable destruction has gone far enough, the equivalent of a "Putin" emerges with a hard core minority of dedicated support often drawn from mid-level and bureaucrats from the bowels of whatever passes for what we call the DOJ and the deep intelligence community. They eat the seniors (heart attacks, strokes, travel accidents and assignations) and buy off existing military from middle levels with advancement and privilege in exchange for absolute loyalty. The oligarchs are never completely defeated, but are battled down to an uneasy stand off and relative subservience. Classic examples of the career bureaucrats, although he is a caricature, are people like Fauci. His only real skill is mastery of the bureaucratic power game. Ultimately, they are forced out one way or another and the structures fall in line for a while. Military becomes a combination welfare program and police force with no moral or ethical structure beyond discipline. Time and again, a small determined core develops enough support to defeat the mightiest army in the absence of any moral fabric and that's where the USA is today – waiting for its American Putin as it slides down to chaos. In every case, there is a corrupt "judicial" system and always the fiction of something like a Constitution, which ours has now become. And the sad part is that the younger players, lacking education and experience, don't understand the Masters they serve or even that they are serving them.

So where is Freemasonry in this? At its best it is staged training and indoctrination system like all the rest. It is based on amoral fabric that many but most certainly not all believe is universal truth. At best, we teach self-discipline in adhering the code of ethics derived from the Morality System. As with all such systems, the leadership is far more often characterized by self-service and hierocracy rather than a genuine desire to serve, and few are willing to understand enough to actually teach. And so we say we lead by example even though the example is often poor at best. Like it or not, our Fraternity follows the same pattern as our culture with a vague hope that we will impact the future.

"Too soon old and too late smart."

The Construct of FM∴

Operative Masonry: from which figure, strength, beauty in architecture, and the just proportion to all of its parts will be derived. In order to understand the purpose for the formation or the development of FM∴ we must first take a look at the events in which the construct of FM∴ came into being.

"Behold, the heaven and heaven of heavens cannot contain thee; how much less this house that I have builded" (Kings 8; 27). We can all agree that the greatest of all construction in every part of the world was brought into the light of day by men who had a vision or a dream, and in that state of consciousness, God spoke to them.

But those dreams came to kings, not to the everyday man, and since only the king could afford to have anything built for them, the architect found a banker for his ideas and innovations. It was in fact these very architects that set in motion the monuments that we still see today and the ones that archeologists are still finding everywhere on the planet in modern times. Every king had an architect, and we can trace this back to the Egyptians, and before them to the Phoenicians and perhaps before them to the Minoans.

Queen Hatshepsut may have had access to the writings of the prophets, but Akhenaten, the Egyptian king who founded his own religion, had an architect named Bek, who was his chief architect. The Egyptians had a principle goddess of architecture named Seshat, also known as the "lady of the builders," of writing, and of the House of the Books. Seshat assisted the king in the laying out of new construction through a ritual act of driving a tall stake into the ground with a mallet. She was at times replaced by Thot, the god of science, or Ptah, the god of crafts.

(Most FM∴ are convinced that mysticism played an important role in the formation of our organization, and to some FM∴ the rituals are rooted in a secret mystery that is up to them to solve, even if it takes them a life time. There is an idea that all individuals should practice the practical art of magic, ritual, and meditation. We need a definition of the word "magic" here. To the average reader, even an educated reader, the word has a different meaning than it once had. It was once a term that simply meant that which we know but do not understand. It is now synonymous with deception or sleight of hand. That is a miscommunication of what was intended when the word was used in early ritual from almost any source.

But these practices must be done in a scientific fashion; they are to be done as a research project into the part of the mind that is the most creative. If it were not for the practice of ritualistic magic, nothing we see of the past as far as building is concerned would have come into being. Nothing built by the ancients was for fun, it all had a purpose, and that purpose was magical, spiritual, and of a state of consciousness that most human beings are unable to comprehend in modern times. But magic and spiritualism are nothing more than a stepping stone in both ancient and modern FM∴. In the past, our ancient brethren believed that this was the only way to god; today, we know more about god, and man.)

We all are creatures of habit, and it must be stated that we do not necessarily evolve with time, nor perhaps is there such a thing as time when measured by the human mind. What we have become in the past 17 years is what will remain of our society if it is to continue. There are changes within the construct of our society that change even the way FM∴ will view itself and how the rest of the world will view FM∴ for that matter. This of course will be taken into consideration if indeed FM∴ is at all important to society to begin with … I for one do not believe that it is. Although I would argue that what its basis is and what was intended by it actually is vital to humanity.

What the architects had built was so sacred that the Egyptians kept records of every building, whether it was for worshipping or for social gatherings. The records of the architects were kept for future use and for future reference. From Thot, the god of science, or Ptah, the god of Craft; a concentration of teachers that envelopes the scope of architecture, from theory to practical knowhow of construction on the other. Imhotep, who was a chief official in Egyptian times, was also the chief head of the cult of Ptah. In the Ptolemaic era, there are legends that Imhotep wrote books on the foundation of temples; these books had to be read by the kings and priests of Egypt before any building of a sacred structure was to be erected as part of their official religion at the time. When reading about these legends, one cannot help but be carried away by the mysticism that surrounds Imhotep. He becomes a being sent down from the heavens to give knowledge of all sorts to the kings and priests of Egypt. But it was this sacred, magical, and mystical expression that became the foundation or the construct of those societies. And these societies would not have grown if the magic and the mysticism had not been the leading factor in the architectural designs as well as the religious ideology of the ancients.

(When we talk about ancient buildings, and it matters not where on the planet we refer our discussion or questions to, nothing was built without the use of slavery. The hired worker was either the taskmaster or the architect himself. A handful of individuals were paid well for their efforts and also carried a great deal of responsibility—as the failure of any of these temples would have spelled death for those in charge of its building. However, the brute work was done mostly by slaves, not volunteers. To feed and house these slaves would have cost any society dearly. And there is no doubt that the use of such methods was taken all the way into the modern era, as slavery held strong up until the late 18th century. With time, it became apparent not just to the slave, but to the chief architects, the taskmasters, the apprentice, the fellow craft, and the Master Mason that slavery as a means of erecting a temple was the downfall of the Egyptian religion itself. When I speak of temples I am not referring to a physical temple, because everything physical in this world has a shelf life.)

Questions may have abounded in the slaves as to why the gods, or the gods of the religions at the time, had selected them and only them as the slaves, and the others as their head masters. With time, the alien religion and culture of Egypt became another chapter in its history. As the time passed, Egypt and its alien culture disappeared. Every aspect of architecture, whether it was the surveying and the surveyors, the stone cutters, the foundation layers, the astronomers who laid some of these structures in line with the stars, the priest, or the kingship, all of these groups with no exception formed their own tribe, clan, craft, later to be refined by the Greeks and

Romans as lodges, and colleges. What we call today Blue Lodge in the FM∴, Odd Fellows Lodges, Pythian Lodges, Knights of Columbus Lodges, the Moose, the Elks, everyone you can think of ... the idea is as old as Egypt herself, because Egypt is the mother of all these principles and ideas. But it does not mean that these ideas where only found in Egypt; it's just that Egypt is located in a certain part of the world where when one measures its location and compares the other structures in other parts of the world, one can only conclude that it had to start there, since everywhere else the buildings are apparently much younger. This statement of course can only hold truth if we are to set our complete trust in the modern system of dating stones, and civilizations, and if we are to trust in this data given to us by professionals from all walks of life. If, however, our society has decided to rewrite history from its very conception with the intent on building another, then indeed we are lost, and so too is our past. I am not one to say, but it is rather speculative that around 500 BC every civilization that had any inclination of architecture was building monumental stone structures in places where there was no communication between civilizations, nor was there any means of commerce or trade being taken. There was no communication with the builders of pyramid shaped structures in Central and South America with known civilizations such as Greece, Rome, or Egypt. Many have speculated that China entered Central and South America, but there too is no definitive truth in that either. Also, why would the Chinese come to Central and South America and not leave their mark on the architecture of these countries? The process used in masonry/concrete/stone cutting, by the ancient civilizations of Latin America was similar to the techniques used by the Romans, Greeks, and Egyptians … how did they learn this with no outside help or influence. This may be less absolute than it seems. One of the wonderful things about archeology is that advancements in our technical has given us the ability to "unearth" our unknown history that suggests connectivity by some intriguing findings in the last decade.

There is one hint of evidence by which these crafts could have traveled farther than most scholars believe. The Greeks, unlike the Egyptians, did not make it a habit to write the names of the architects down on their monuments, nor where there, nor has there ever been discovered a book from ancient Greece that details the methods used by the architects to design and build their temples and social buildings. Because, by the time of Greece, one of those crafts that I had previously mentioned had already become a working lodge, and its builders where no longer architects. They were craftsmen themselves; in other words, they designed as they built. There were no architectural drawings, no foundation expert; these were master tradesmen. They knew the work from top to bottom and thought it best to keep the trade a secret by not creating drawings that could be used by others and eventually lead to the end of the craftsmen themselves.

(The end of craftsmanship came eventually, as machines took the place of human hands, and architects sat in offices in rooms where several hundred of them worked on different parts of the completion of a plane, a house, a ship, and the factories that made them, right down to the machinery that makes the machinery to build everything we see today. The craftsman became obsolete, driven into obscurity just as had been the case with the ancient gods of Egypt, Greece, Rome, and elsewhere on the planet.)

Everything serves a purpose, and the Greek term *architekton* meant, at least initially, nothing more than master carpenter, rather than master architect. The Greek method was different; the master craftsman was allowed to settle architectural design on site. The stone mason in Greek times worked in worded detailed instructions on design set by the architect, and they are referred to as "syngraphia." The instructions on the building of certain structures in Greece were nothing more than an order of how things were to be made, transported, and erected. However, the methods used to carve, cut, stamp, or assemble these monuments are nowhere to be found because the craftsmen had by this time established their own trade secrets, and these trade secrets became the backbone of what the Egyptians had as a mystical, religious philosophy of building. By the time the Greeks were building in wood and stone, the idea of a traveling craftsmen was already in order. The craftsmen involved in traveling to a certain part of Greece to look for a certain craftsman who quarried a particular stone that was needed to erect a temple, some 200 kilometers away is what would have been called in Egyptian times the architect. By the time the Greeks were building with stone, the stone masons had already discovered their craft and were doing this for a profit, not for the love of the art, and most certainly not for the love of a religion. All of the financing was provided by the city states. What was built for private individuals of the aristocracy was paid by that individual himself. And most likely this is where the idea of designers came about, since the wealthy could afford to pay the craftsmen, the wealthy would design their own vision of what they wanted to see. Eventually, you have someone who has a vision, but does not know how to make it a reality. That visionary seeks the help of an architect, and the architect seeks the help of a craftsmen to build it. This only held true until the 20th century, when the contractor came into being, and the craftsmen was no longer the designer, architect, and builder of a project. This was the manner in which civilizations thrived for centuries, and also the manner in which some of the most spectacular monuments of mankind have been created. And today more than ever we see it as massive consulting companies take an idea and develop it stem to stern on behalf of the client or corporation by who they have been retained, utilizing specialized technology that is not cost effective as a one off.

(The Sears tower and other large buildings across the world today are also monuments that could not be achieved by just a simple craftsman. It involves engineering on a scale that was not thought of before. All this means is that the crafts-man's trade became so complex that it needed to divide the load in order to continue building. Society itself has changed. We can see from a historical point of view that it was a priestly society, and a society of Kings and Queens that made the architects branch out into craftsmen, and those craftsmen ventured wherever the wind would carry them, and they too laid the foundations of other societies. Very, very few craftsmen wrote their legacy or their names into history books, and as we shall see in the following pages, the arrival of a new lodge, or college of craftsmen that took our society as well as the society in every part of the world into the new era of building and the structuring of a nation and/or nations.)

The Middle Ages—which cover a period from about the second half of the Fifth Century to the first half of the 15th century according to historians was tagged "ex post facto" by individuals hesitant to proclaim their own understanding of everything including nature itself. This was not something our ancient brethren, the craftsmen, reflected upon. This was an era of reflection. Much of it—and some historians will disagree with this statement—relates to man's fundamental attraction to music and the building of very large cathedrals where this music could be appreciated. Music was not considered a science at the time, but rather a gift from God to man by which man could express his desires to not only be with God but also to reflect on the Creator's work, and also for the creation to reflect on the work they were able to do because of this gift. Music was a way to adorn the Temples on a philosophical level, not on a visual level. I am not going to get into the vocalization of mantras, or the Gothic spires or hovels of earlier, more primitive, methods of reaching the gods via the vocalization of sounds. In the first century of history— the history that is taught in schools today—Christianity emphasized on the value of "individualism" with limitations. In theory, every individual had a place, and that individual had duties. My focus on this era is not with the history of the era, but rather with the individuals who gave others a "duty" and a "place" in society. Without it, society would have never gone any further.

(This was a point in time when society was going through a growing pain; hence, the 10 centuries spanned by the Middle Ages can be divided into two sections: the first section, as with many of the FM∴ rituals, is a section of chaos and torpor. The second section is a time of growing stability, purposeful organizations and institutions, as well as the awakening or the opening of the eyes of the individual. After much war and distraction, the more pagan societies turned their attention toward the new-found faith. All historians will agree on this, yet none will give an explanation on how whoever kills another in order to make them believe in something else is in fact not progress, but a simple change of authority. Hence, societies that had flourished in architecture became the societies that changed history if not created history to begin with. Places like Poland and Denmark and Hungary became examples of the forward-looking Christian states within a few decades of their "leaders" changing faith. Remember that we said the Egyptians had "taskmasters." Here, you will see that nothing had changed in the order of governing society, but rather what changed was the way society views those who are giving them these "tasks" in which they are about to receive, but not without conflict—since it became necessary to kill millions upon millions of people in order to make this change.)

By the end of WWI, FM∴ had been a center of thought—a think tank, or brain box as they were called back during this time, that had been around for over 300 years. But we are going to go back to the 16th and 17th century to see how this think tank grew and what it did to change the way the world viewed freedom and the rights and liberties of the people that make up the world. One of the oldest known and documented ceremonies performed on a candidate can be traced back to 1645, and it was the passing to the degree of fellow craft for a member in England. By 1717, the first grand lodge of FM∴ was formed in England, and by that time period, most of the guildsmen who were part of a trade union had won their freedom from their lords by means of working for their freedom. These guildsmen became prominent members of this newly found gentlemen's club called FM∴. The ideas that were discussed ranged from science to architecture, philosophy to politics, and the rules of law and government.

It was here and during this time period that FM∴ became a sort of revolution, and by the late 16th century, there were lodges in England, France, Germany, Spain, and eventually America. It is a strange coincidence that all of these nations went through some sort of revolution, and it was due mostly to the introduction of a type of philosophy that is prominent in FM∴: the respect for law and order, the acknowledgement of the rights and freedom of each and every individual, and most of all, a strict moral conduct. None of these attributes were prominent in the religious institutions at the time, and even less so in the ruling class such as the kingships of these countries. For the most part, kings were sovereign entities sent down from the gods, and the church supported them so long as the kingship acknowledged the power of the church. For the most part, the average human being was nothing more than a piece of meat that could be traded for a loaf of bread if need be. The lower class, if indeed there was such a thing during this time period, took a back seat, and had to wait another 100 years before they were acknowledged as human beings with equal rights and privileges. In the Caribbean islands, FM∴ led a small group of men to free themselves from the clutches of Spain and her monarchs. The acts of despotism by the Spanish crown on the people of these small islands was so intolerable that these small islands found support for their revolutions in the U.S. FM∴ was a sort of highway for anyone who was a member seeking to better himself and his nation. Of course, we are talking about a time where there was such a thing as a martyr, a person who would lay down his or her life in order to save or preserve a way of life for others, with a love for their country unlike what we see today. And support or money was not in a form of a weekly check; it came in bits and pieces from wealthy individuals who also had a vision for those small island states. The philosophy of Kant, Hume, Locke, and Swedenborg, were read by the intellectuals who led these revolutions, and more importantly the history of the past which they never lost sight of.

Anyone with a well-equipped library can find this information and trace it back to wherever their heart desires. My intentions are to spend only the needed amount of time to explain a construct that has been enveloped in mystery and conspiracy—all of which is a fantasy written by creative writers to make sensational out of that which is not, FM∴ is historical at best, not sensational. Taken as a commentary on most if not almost all contemporary writing on Freemasonry, the criticism is intended.

FM∴ was the stepping stone for something much bigger than most would agree to, but its reality is much more interesting than its fiction. As the craftsman who gained his freedom by the forbidden knowledge of building, to the guildsman who later formed the lodges, to the think tank that it later on turned into, the ideas of Labor Unions, the 8-hour work day, and the method by which we pay wages, all of this came from think tanks such as FM∴ not from the church, not from the kingship, and most certainly not by the governments at the time period. It may come as a surprise to most today, since most individuals do very little reading, that in this nation we had, at one time, child labor, and those laws did not become laws until the think tanks and their members created them. It was not unusual for the Federal Government to send troops to force miners to go back to work for the wages that the owners of these mines were inclined to pay. This history is also available at the public library with a well-stocked collection of books on the industrial revolution and labor laws. The laws of our nation were decided mostly by a group not unlike Mafiosi who at the time called themselves statesmen. One needs only to study the time periods of the 20's and 30's to understand that our nation is owned by a few families, and it's the distribution of wealth, and how we as a society *view* wealth that has made any changes in our society at the present time.

By the start of WWII, our nation had been led by several prominent FM∴, and as we say, FM∴ is perfect, but Masons themselves are not always perfect. The end of WWII brought in a different sort of think tank, and by the early 50's and 60's FM∴ began to see a sudden drop in membership.

The loss of membership in FM∴ as well as the other fraternities such as the Odd Fellows, the Pythians, the Elks, the Moose, etc. was not just do to the advent of television and other activities that were abundant during this time period. It was largely due to the fact that most Masonic lodges, or fraternities that practiced Masonic forms of initiation and conduct were no longer discussing the issues that were once upon a time important.

(At its most humble beginnings, the purpose for the formation of an organization such as the FM∴ is not for the simple act of preserving some ancient rite of passage by performing rituals that are said to be 100's of years old, nor was it to keep the secrets of architecture from those who were not members of a trade or preserve a way of life. It was formed to teach through a degree process that what we learn, teach, practice, and preach is not ours, but rather it belonged to those who came before us. And the respect we pay to those who came before us in Masonic ritual is not something that is practiced by any other entity or organization such as church or government. And I will reemphasize: it is simply a way to show respect for those who came before us, be it a god, or a creature of god. This type of respect is not considered by any standards normal. By our masonic standards its considered a moral act. And we prefer it to be as such—a moral act of respect for others who came before us, as King Solomon said, "there is nothing new under the sun.")

It would be illogical if not stupid to think that FM∴ was developed during the enlightenment era by a group of wealthy individuals who enjoyed the theatrics of ancient historical events, or a social club for old men with nothing to do. FM∴ had a deep purpose at one time, and these were revolutionary times, where the freedom of men and the respect of the creature—man—was put before anything.

Not even the religious organizations at that time period considered mankind worth serving or saving, neither did the kingship or government at the time. Human life was to serve a purpose, and that purpose was to fulfill the needs and desires, capricious or not, of the ruling class and the institutions that formed them. What FM∴ did was make everyone human; there are no, and there never were any, gods amongst FM∴. As one 33' Mason once put it, "we are the only organization in which its masters step down every year, and another takes his place, with no arguments, and there is no discord amongst the members as in any social organization, discord can and does occur. The further we stray from our roots, the more it becomes normalized and procedural. Within this context, we have strayed far from what we were and ought to be. But it's what we preach—friendship, charity, and brotherly love for one another ... a kindled respect for human life and what the creature man has made with the help of God."

By the end of the 60's and into the early 70's, FM∴ took a back seat in the think tank movement. No longer were FM∴

involved as a fraternity in the aspect of society, economics, politics, and philosophy. The American Masonic institution became more of a charity organization and much less a think tank. (I am not saying that some FM∴ didn't remain part of think tanks, and some may have been members of many think tanks, but the fraternity itself no longer was a stronghold for information and innovation.) What happened next was a struggle for perfection of the degree work. Many of the new officers during the 70's were sticklers for memory work, and the memorization of lectures that lasted up to an hour were expected to be done by rote memory. This became a stumbling block for the fraternity, for many of its members were in the age bracket of 60-70 years, and the younger generation was simply not interested in the theatrics and the mysteries. This became apparent to any member after he had seen one or two degrees performed and had spent 1 year in the organization. Institutions such as the Rosicrucian, the Golden Dawn, the Gnostics became a place where the younger generation wanted to be— the spiritual awakening that was not taught in FM lodges.

Though countless symposiums and articles had been written and entertained by the appendant body of York Rite Masonry—The Allied Masonic Degrees—the mystical and spiritual part of the lectures were too difficult to communicate to the younger member. The term "instant gratification" had seemed to take a hold of society, and everyone wanted answers, and when they did not find them in the institution, they went elsewhere; more often than not, the elsewhere was not so well informed either.

By the early 80's, the publication of books such as Holy Blood, Holy Grail came out, and made some connection between folklore and fact. The connecting of the Knights Templar with the Free Masons put the fraternity back on track with membership. But it was not until 2003 that Dan Brown published his whopping story of a blood line of Christ, the female goddess and the shaping of the Templars into a cult that worshiped the female dominance, or the worshipping of Mary of Mandela. A mystical organization called the Priory of Zion practiced ritual magic and worshiped goddesses as well as kept secrets of the highest value claiming to poses a secret that can be scandalous to any religious organization. The worst of the matter is that most who read the book, concluded it was true, because the fantasy was much greater than the truth. By in large, even while I sat in Church on Sunday to hear the priest after mass proclaim, that he too had read the Da Vinci Code and that the story was not true. The fact that the priest brought it up on his own gave me the inclination that the idea had been discussed amongst the clergy for some time.

What the Da Vinci Code did for FM∴ was that it brought in a few additional young individuals seeking to know the secrets of the Templars and the other orders that were still a mystery to them. For the record: there is no proof that Free Masonry or Frank Masonry had anything to do with the Knights Templar. The Templar Knight was one of many orders the Church created. As far as I have been able to investigate, there were some 54 military orders within in the Church; many were created by prominent members of society: Lords, kings, and nobles who defended a town from the Moors and formed an order of their own. In Spain this was a common practice and the membership in these organizations or appendant bodies of the church were kept small. You might be talking about 20-30 members per organization. These were not think tanks per se, but they could have acted as a barometer for the city states that at the time. The only means of communication was by letter, and the means of delivering that letter was on horseback.

The history of medieval Spain begins with the Iberian Kingdom of the Arianist Visigoths (507–711) who were converted to Catholicism with their king Rec-cared in 587. Visigoth culture in Spain can be seen as a phenomenon of late antiquity as much as part of the Age of Migrations.

The history of Spain is marked by waves of conquerors that brought distinct cultures to the peninsula. After the passage of the Vandals and Alans down the Mediterranean coast of Hispania around 408 AD and the Muslims From Northern Africa in 711 AD, the Muslim Umayyad dynasty entered Europe and sparked a Muslim versus Christian war called the Reconquista, or the Reconquest (i.e.: The Christians "reconquering" their lands as a religious crusade). Their point of entry was the Strait of Gibraltar, and the soldiers spread from modern day Portugal and Spain to southern France in 10 years.

Francisco Verdugo was a member of a military order called the Order of Santiago, or Saint James, which cannot be understood outside of the context of the Military Orders of Knighthood. Historians seem to be conflicted as to whether Knights in Spanish were directed more by Castilian and Catalan-Aragonese royalty or by the Papacy. (I am using Spain as an example for the French Templars who seem to be an enigma to most historians—mostly those on made-for-television documentaries). But there seems to be a consensus that the knights had obligations to both and an overarching allegiance to the Church, as both were in direct contact with knights (and often royalty were themselves knights and Crusaders). Some suggest that the later Spanish Military Orders, like that at the Fortress of Calatrava, pledged their loyalty primarily to their Kingdom, in this case Castile, but orders like the Templars or Hospitallers were more independent and not necessarily loyal to any kingdom consistently.

In Spain the Christian knights and kingdoms were engaged with what was almost universally acknowledged as a foe to Christianity, and this common enemy had some role in uniting Christian kingdoms in the cause of the Crusades and

Reconquista. Most of the prominent Spanish knightly orders were founded in the early stages of formation, between the 12th and13[th] century. The early formation of the Orders of the peninsula was dangerous and unstable. In Calatrava during the middle of the 12th century, Castilian Knights established a fortress, which would later be abandoned due to the threat of Muslim attack, then again within fifty years a fort of the Order of Calatrava was rebuilt and became a fortified monastic community.

In 1053, the battle of Civitate (Knights of Saint Peter) was begun by Pope Leo IX to counter the Normans. The Knights Templar was founded in 1118. The first secularized order was the Order of Saint George (1326) by Charles of Hungary, who made the Hungarian nobility swear loyalty to him. The second secular order was the Knights of the Band founded in 1332 by King Alfonso XI of Castile. The purpose for the formation of these knightly orders was a combination of religious and military purposes. The Knights Hospitaller and the Knights of Saint Thomas had charitable purposes. They cared for the poor and the sick. One significant feature of the military orders is that clerical bothers could be, and indeed were, subordinate of non-ordained brothers. In 1820, José Antonio Conde suggested that they were molded on the "Ribat," a fortified religious institution which brought together a religious and hospital way of life with fighting the enemy—Islam. The Majority of the military orders' members were layman. They provided a conduit for cultural and technological innovations. Because of the necessity of a standing army, the military orders were founded, being adopted as the fourth monastic religious vows. The first order to appear in Spain was the order of Calatrava in Castile in 1158, followed by the order of Santiago founded in Cáceres, in the Leonese Kingdom in 1170. Six years later, the Order of Alcántara initially called Julian Del Peseiro. The last appearing Order of Montesa did later on during the 14th century in the crown of Aragon due to the dissolution of the order of the Temple. The Master of the order was the absolute power militarily, politically, or religiously. The masters were chosen by a council of 13 friars. The master was installed for life and could by incapacity or pernicious conduct be removed from the order. The political-military was divided into "major encomiendas." Their greater encomienda was in each peninsula, or kingdom, in which was present the order in question. In front of them was the commander followed by the encomiendas, which were a set of goods, not always territorial nor grouped, but generally constituted territorial demarcations. The encomiendas were administered by a commander that was headed by an arcade appointed by the commander. The religious groups or orders were organized by the convents, of which the main convent was the headquarters of the order. The recruitment of members was due to the encomienda's constitution. Presumably, each had a member of liaisons, or men related to the economic value of the demarcation.

Note: the surprising bellicosity of the orders was due to the many continuations of authentic "private wars" against the Muslims when, for various reasons, the Christian King gave up the struggle because of signing truces or to direct his military action in another way.

We see that in Spain the military Christian Orders were abundant, and they were started by small groups of men who happen to be nobles. Some of them took arms against the Muslims because they had lost territories and were paying taxes for a land that belonged to them, and not to the Muslims. But these Knights, or Military Christian Orders, did not take orders from a King or from the Church. It was under their own discretion as to whom they were going to pay their homage. For the most part, they were led by a code of monastic belief systems. I do not necessarily believe that the intent was always honorable, since many times they engaged in their own private wars.

The Crusades came 400 years too late, but when they did, the crusades did what the Moors did when they concurred with these European countries: they taxed the heck out of the people and used that money to finance a military and of course themselves. The crusades were no different than an organized army, and in fact, it's what lead to an organized army. We need to remember that those who walked along dark water-fronts in the late 12th century did so with step and a concealed dagger. Long had the Mediterranean coast of France, Italy, and Spain been areas into which no Christian ventured after dark without arms and a prayer in heart. And as the century drew to its close, the danger increased due to the many Muslim pirates of North Africa becoming increasingly bold. To the rescue of those who were used by the pirates as a means of operational cost and were held as slaves to be sold or bartered for ransom, came the

Order of the Most Holy Trinity. If the governments of Europe would do nothing to rescue those captured by pirates, then the holy Felix of the royal line of Valois would be reminded, for he prayed for guidance, and at the age of 22 gathered all of his worldly possessions and renouncing them retired in hermitage near Meaux in search of God. At about the same time, a young, brilliant doctor at a University of Paris, John de Matha, who was just ordained a priest was thinking the same thing. And after having a vision of Christ with with a cross, a Christian slave at his right hand, and a Moor at his left, John de Matha found one meaning: he had to rescue those Christians taken as slaves by the Moors in Algeria. After John de Matha withdrew from his asylum, he met with the noble Felix. The two had a single aim; it was to gather a group of men about them who, through prayer and exhortation, would arouse the conscience of France, effecting the release of these Christian captives. It took 5 years for this organization to be fruitful and to be able to travel to Rome which, in around 1198, sought the approbation of their order. Pope Innocent granted his approval on December 17th of that year. Like this story, which is documented in history, there are many others.

It is to no surprise that during the 12th and 13th century, what came out of the Christian movement was not just the Inquisition, which killed thousands depending on whose view of the Inquisition you read, but also an army, a banking system, an economical map of sorts, and a set of virtues by which to live. Yes, we can say that the clergy and the feudalist rulers and their quest for power and dominance destroyed much of our history and replaced it with another. But it gave rise to the Christian men and woman who would dedicate their lives to instances that they perceived to be messages from God. Orders such as the Congregation of the Blessed Sacrament and the Congregation of the Holy Cross, best known in the U.S. for its Notre Dame University of Indiana. It had its beginnings in 1837 in the town of Le Mans, Northwestern France. The roots for this organization were founded by Father Francois Dujarié and the genius of Father Basile Moreau. These organizations were formed by men of the clergy who saw the aftermath of the French Revolution and witnessed the chaos in education wrought by the governments interdict upon religious schools. By reading of these organizations, we see that the Crusades were just the start of a new era. Later, as government and church separated, there were still other wars to be fought. These wars were still religious and political in nature. The enemy became everyone, and as the church fought with the growing powers that came out of the Crusades, we see a lot of dust, and it is difficult to see what happened, but one thing is for certain: both the clergy and the decedents of those noble men who took up arms against a common enemy found their place in society. There is no doubt that many prominent individuals in society have joined our fraternity—the Free Masons, but it is highly unlikely that Free Masonry came before them as an organized institution. Someone had to plow the field before another could plant the seeds.

Reality and Fiction

The Free Masons were not Templars, and the Templars were not Free Masons. The Templars were disbanded some 300 before the creation of a fraternity calling itself Free Masonry. I believe that York Rites Masonry adopted the Templar Order due to its persistency and zeal for honor, truth, and integrity, but most of all, due to the love of Christianity which was tied to a large population during the formation of all the Masonic bodies. It would only be appropriate for an organization which works as a science not to adopt the leading religion at the time period from which it was conceived. It also adopted the Order of Malta, which offered charity and aid for the sick and poor. The Masonic institution practiced many sciences, and charity was one of them.

The very real history of the Templar Knights as it played out into today is a fascinating subject even without the baseless fictions so often presented as fact. Any casual student with a little initiative can sort that one out. There are discoveries yet to be made. The connectivity from English Templars to the Knights of St. Thomas of Acon and then to the Mercers of today is attracting credible academic attention and fun to see it unfold. But, the mystery of the Templar Knights is a creation of fiction. Since it is difficult to explain such a devotion to an institution, such as with the Templar, the Order of Malta, and others, the best way to describe this devotion to the service of God is quite simple. Christianity is a supernatural religion. And when the Templars fought, they fought with the courage of 100 men. This made them a legend amongst their enemies, and since they only had one real enemy—the Muslims—and one real institution to please—the Catholic Church, life was quite simple. But the lives these individuals endured as Templar Knights were by no means pleasant. A life of sacrifice and devotion is not a life of romance, but it is the stuff that romance novels are based on.

As the years have passed and we sit in a lodge in America in the year 2017, we see again that for most of us who have stayed long enough to see the changes, FM∴ has lost touch with its members and its needs. Today, keeping a lodge open is no different than a small mom and pop shop trying to compete with Wall Mart or K Mart. Membership is at an all-time low, and it's not because we lack interest, it's because we have in fact served a purpose, but that purpose we no longer wish to serve because it may not be politically correct. Although there are a few noteworthy exceptions, the older masons are dying out, and those that are still hanging on can barely keep up. It is like the Templar Knight in the movie Indiana Jones where the Templar Knight guarding the holy grail could barely pick up his sword to swing it, his strength gone, but the love for the fight, continues on till his death. And so too are we.

There is one light left in Masonry, and it is called the AMD—a small think tank devoted only to the research papers and lectures that its members bring to any MM∴ who desires to attend when not holding a closed meeting. A group consisting of no more than 26 members per council, and with 17 councils across the state of Florida for instance, you can expect some very interesting papers will come out of there. This organization is by invitation only, and those invited to join are usually pleased that they were looked upon as someone who could add to the subject. That subject will be later explained. For those who are invited, the construct of FM∴ may indeed be revealed where there are knowledgeable members available on the various aspects of our ritual, mystery, and yes - magic. is reviled.

(The FM∴ that I am referring to in this paper, is American FM∴, not to be confused with European FM∴ or Latin American FM∴ because the they are not remotely the same although FM∴ in England may have drifted away as it has in America. They function differently and have an entirely different agenda than ours in America. In this paper, I will not go into the European or Latin American FM∴)

The Anteroom

This is the room before the lodge; this is the place in your mind where you are trapped in the world around you. In this room, your mind is free to roam, and your thoughts are free to be expressed. Always avoiding discord and assertions amongst your peers—and these are your peers, not the ones selected for a jury pool. Your peers are your bothers, and anyone who is a FM∴ knows the difference between the two, and most will tell you they have no peers, just brothers.

In this room, we will discuss the construct of FM∴ and its true purpose, and the vials that it has created in order to remain anonymous, but as the clock ticks and time passes, it's time to learn what we are about. However, before I begin, there are certain rules that will be obeyed, and if you do not like the rules you can find another way to get your answers … After all, there is more than one way to skin a cat.

Rule #1) The secret of the order that pertains to its ceremonies will not be discussed because they are not only relevant to the formation of the organization, and how the institution conducts its method of teaching. They are complex, in-volved—a combination of times and places, and many times the time period does not match the event; sometimes the event never took place … it's metaphorical. These are called the philosophical degrees or the higher degrees. I will not discuss ceremonial work.

Rule #2) The involvement of FM∴ in any of the arguments that is related to modern think tanks may be purely coincidental because FM∴ has not been a think tank for many years, so to conclude that the information I am about to give is created, governed, or directed by any Masonic Fraternity is unfounded. Therefore, the reader will consider this as one of the reasons fraternities such as ours came into being, but not the sole purpose for its existence.

Free Masonry is a science, and like all sciences, it is to be studied. It envelops art, music, literature, mathematics, geometry, language, and philosophy. Since it is a complete science, FM∴ and Free Masons have been known to work with the magical arts, the effects of music, and the power of geometry. Philosophy came later on, but notwithstanding the philosophy of ancient times, most of what was left of the library of Alexandria is the works of Socrates, Plato, and Aristotle. Our philosophy is limited to European work; later on, we have Thomas Paine, Kant, Hume, Locke, and others. All of which worked off the efforts of the earlier philosophers, and they (the earlier philosophers) did the same. In essence, someone taught someone else, and so on. But somewhere there had to have been a seed of light, and that seed turned on an entire sky full of light. How that light is distributed is unknown to anyone, but our early Greek and Egyptian philosophers pondered on these ideas. Hammering like a blacksmith on a subject instead of a piece of steel, the philosopher eventually molds his mind and the minds of others into a tool—a tool that can be used for both good and evil.

It is very difficult and also a major undertaking to try to explain our economy, even though there are many courses you can take at a local college on the subject. When one studies economics, it appears that there are certain guidelines that have to be followed; however, when you consider that our economy works almost by magic, you get a different feel for it. To some, our economy is like a casino. To others, our economy is based on mathematical models that are carefully laid out, and still there are flaws.

How can it be that there is a flaw in a mathematical model? Human nature is something that cannot be predicted 100% of the time. One can come close, but never reach that goal. What if one could control the circumstances, however? What if one could make a problem and at the same time create the solution? Could one easily control human nature? Perhaps if one could create different mathematical equations that would work simultaneously with other mathematical models, and all one had to do is change the models for each situation, could human nature be controlled by the use of such methods?

We will examine this mathematical theory by looking at the think tanks of our modern day, and we can decide if we are to continue believing that we live by chance and luck, or by the creation of ideas and innovations, and, also who comes up with the idea, and how far will it be allowed to proceed.

We will begin with the RAND Corporation and some of its topics of interest. I will only touch on the topics of interest of these modern day think tanks. I will not go in depth because to do so would require thousands of pages of information, and no one is going to sit down and read thousands of pages of information to get an idea of what is happening around them.

"He that knows others is a man of wit, but he who knows himself is truly illuminated." Think tanks are a diverse institution that vary in size, financing, structure, and scope of activity. There are currently well over 1,500 think tanks or political research centers in the U.S.—around half of which are university affiliated institutions, and about one third of which are located in Washington, D.C. Those think tanks that are not affiliated with academic institutions, political parties, or special interest groups are described as freestanding or independent think tanks. Since the '80s, the majority of the think tanks established have focused on issues concerning global warming, public policy, and national security. 25 out of the 30 top think tanks in the U.S. focus on a wide range of topics both domestic and international. Factors that lead to the formation of these think tanks are:

- Division of power between the three branches of government and the level of government (state and federal)
- Political systems that have weak political parties that exhibit little or no party discipline
- Highly developed philanthropic and civil culture
- Public that has a healthy distrust of government and prefers a limited role for government

- Proclivity of citizens to join and support interest groups rather than political parties to represent their interest and express their policy preferences
- Political system that has many points of access
- Tendency to embrace independent experts over politicians or bureaucrats

The political and philosophical foundations of think tanks can affect not only the perspective from which research is conducted, but also its outcome. Some think tanks offer forthright explanations of their ideological bent, while others prefer to maintain at least the appearance of nonpartisanship, based on their self-expressed political or philosophical orientation, the orientation of their associated scholars, and their sponsored publications. At one end of this spectrum are the conservative think tanks, which generally espouse both a free market economic policy and a traditionalist social policy. Libertarian think tanks are similar, yet their emphasis on laissez-faire economics is primary, and the government's role in social policy is discouraged. The centrist think tanks that exist today are noteworthy for the wide range of their scholars' views and also for their emphasis on a detached and nonpartisan approach to policy that allows for a synthesis of conservative and progressive elements.

Some think tanks that focus on particular fields or issues (e.g. defense and security think tanks) are categorized as conservative or progressive based on the current manifestation of conservative and liberal orientation in those particular fields. Thus, think tanks that follow the realist or neoconservative school in defense and foreign policy are categorized as conservative, while think tanks that generally represent a more liberal internationalist approach are categorized as progressive. The think tank community, regardless of an individual scholar's party affiliation or philosophical orientation, recognizes a scholarly tradition and a commitment to finding the truth and figuring out what is best for the country. Obviously, not every scholar or institution adheres to these standards 100% of the time, but that is the standard that most think tanks and policy makers have come to expect from the scholars who work at these institutions.

The Rand Institution

RAND came out after the second world war. A five-star general named Henry "Hap" Arnold decided that America needed great minds to keep it safe from all enemies and it needed to be done in order to keep up with technological advances. In 1946, he gathered a group of scientists and with $10 million in funding started RAND, which stands for Research and development. After a few short months, RAND got the attention of academics, military strategists, and politicians by proposing a preliminary design of experimental circulating spaceship. They also predicted that his circulating spaceship would be able to predict weather patterns, and also one day transform long distance communications. Truman passed on the subject, but the military loved it, and with "Hap's" connections the military became RAND's biggest think tank contractor.

RAND also had over 1,000 researchers on board at one time; these individuals would gather information on any given subject. The goal was to see who was developing what, and how they could get ahead of the game with new technologies that were emerging on a geometric rate.

We see in the '40s and prior to that with other think tanks that came much earlier that the target was not necessarily technology but rather economic wealth and how to distribute society into nice, neat little bundles of joy. RAND, by the mid '40s was interested in world communication and also world domination of what is going on—on a global scale. The ancients did something similar, except they called it communications with the gods, and the 10th century, clergy called the kingdom of heaven here on earth, while later on in the 15th-17th centuries, philosophers called it enlightenment … call it what you will, the will of the people has to be monitored and sometimes adjusted; if not, someone else will do the monitoring, and someone else will be in charge. What turns out to be good or bad for everyone is for anyone to say, since the outcome sometimes is worse than what you had. But if it were not for the Christian movement (or rather if it were not for the appearance of Christ, and Christianity), the Jewish people would have been obliterated by the Romans and the Goths who basically believed in nothing, and later on, the despotic if not hasty act of Queen Isabella—who, not for religious reasons, but rather for economic reasons, turned the Spanish Inquisition on to the

Jews who in fact helped her gain power and wealth. After all, this is how one repays those who help when one is the queen.

Although one would like to think that God would have protected the Jews from complete destruction, we cannot help but contemplate on what the difference would have been, had Christianity not developed as one of the favored religions of the Roman Empire, or at all.

From Game Theory to mathematicians who would come up with ways on how to avoid a nuclear disaster by creating fail-safe systems for the nuclear missiles that were being built at the time, RAND did it all. If you think that IBM invented the first computer … think again. Although in actuality, it appears the Egyptians indeed had a metal object that behaved like a mechanical computer and it was used for complex astronomical prediction.

The biggest secret in all of humanity is that we are connected both mentally and spiritually; this connection is what led societies all over the world to build monuments of epic proportions, societies with structured government, and religious belief systems. These societies ruled without communication with one another. Later in the first half of the19[th] century, the thinkers of the world (the brain boxes) figure out this secret or this trait, and it became necessary to form bigger think tanks—think tanks that were much larger than Free Masonry. These think tanks concluded that the connection of every human being with one another would lead to discoveries and innovations as well as technology that—if they were not monitored, censored, or controlled—would undermine the disassociated public or the working class with the ruling class. It would bring the end to all forms of governing bodies. There would not exist such a thing as poverty because it would be indistinguishable from wealth. If it were allowed to continue as it was heading, if the human freethinker was allowed innovations and technology, the advances would be so inexpensive that the world in which we live today and the wars that are fought today would not exist in its current fashion.

Long before Stalin, Hitler, Mussolini, and other despots wrote their names into the history books, the idea of eliminating certain races or clans of people who had a unique capability to communicate ideas and innovations with others had already been dealt with. Those who were able to do this outside of their will simply because they possessed a certain ability (humility, dignity, and integrity) via esoteric meditation or simple prayer, took the ideas far away, without the use of e-mail, telephone, or radio. These races were considered a threat, though at times we want to relate those threats as being economically strong, naturally intelligent, or genuinely selected by the gods to survive and thrive. And this ability can only be explained by those who are capable of doing it and have devoted their lives to this work. I for one am not one of those, but I admire them for their work.

Freemasonry was one of the sciences that was developed early on in the mid-to-late 16th century, but due to barbarianism, this noble think tank took more twists and turns that it eventually became deaf and dumb. Numb to many of the ideas just proposed, FM∴ took a back seat. Today, even though some will speculate that FM∴ is a sleeping giant of a think tank, I would venture to say … not so.

Nonetheless, FM∴ knew from its inception that the people of the past, our ancient brethren, were able to not only communicate ideas with mystical if not ancient processes that later on was developed as a science, they were also able to strive and continue to be here and offer whatever they could in order for humanity to continue on its quest. For those who do not believe in the power of prayer, consider then the scientific terminology of the power of persuasion. For those who do not consider miracles a reality, but just a matter of chance, consider the entire world we live in as a matter of fact. In the beginning there was the word, and the word was with God, and the word was God. All was created with a word. How does an ancient society that had not yet come into the age of enlightenment come up with such an idea? Unless the idea was a vision which was planted in the brain from the very beginning. FM∴ is a science, and we would like to keep it that way, because in this fashion we can put a subject in its hermetic form and analyze each and every thought, word, or concept that may come to mind. It's too bad that FM∴ is no longer the think tank of the old, but rather a memory of the past. We still have hope.

The study of architecture and design became the science of the era; with time, humans—the only species that builds empires—have taken the old system of design and architecture to a new frontier. In furniture building, or design, we have a few segments where we went from the very ornate to the very simple. This too stands as a fact with architectural buildings and architectural furniture. We no longer see the large wall units—those that towered up to the ceilings as if reaching for the heavens. We no longer build furniture with a wood color or a wood grain, although some of what I see today has some grain, but the colors are explicitly white in nature. Everything is square, white, gray, or shades of white and gray. All the wood tones are out except for a few places where a dark color or contrast is needed, but for the most part … it's all square and white in nature.

This tells us a great deal about what is going on in the mind of society. If we are looking for simplicity in architecture, then we are looking for simplicity in design. I believe that the desire of some, if not most, individuals for everything to be white and square has to do with the advent of technology, the simplicity of the task that computers do for us today, and cell phones. The connections we have today is global, but this technology, though advanced and complicated, is presented as simple, square, and white to the public. As everything is square and white, void of curves and angles, and color is non-existent, so too is the imagination of those who live in this net. Most were happy this new design came about, and others simply followed the trend.

This trend of simplicity in design has also passed on to the lowering of standards. Standards that were once the backbone of a society are now lowered for all to reach. Competition is considered taboo and they have hired the mouth of science to prove that competition has stifled if not destroyed lives. A society that cannot connect with its desire to design and build and also be competitive is a society of sheep. Nothing progressive comes out of a society of sheep. There must be a mixture, and we seem to be missing the formula; someone has carelessly lost it. Or we have lost those who had the skill to design and build, and what we are left with is a group of simpletons as with the beginning of all societies.

We build today on a concept of pictures out of a magazine, and then put those pictures together to form a complete concept. The idea of genius is taboo, and intellect is considered dangerous if not monitored or controlled. We see this with technology; we are obsessed with monitoring one another because we do not trust one another anymore then we trust ourselves … at least, this appears to be the modern concept of things. Today, a search engine can determine the outcome of a political election as well as the progress of a student; nothing is left to chance. We have separated classes into subclasses, and when we run out of objectives, society creates them. When one race is targeted too often in a crime, we describe that race as another, similar to, but not the same, in order as to appear unbiased, and to be politically correct. This new construct is much more difficult to describe—let alone analyze, since there is no bases for its existence. We are living in a very dangerous time period. We have sociopaths for leaders, and the very concept of cognitive values are nonexistent. Today, the parents an eight-year-old boy who wants to be recognized as a girl is suing the local school because the school does not allow the eight-year-old to act out a roll as a girl. At eight years of age, a child today is conscious of what sexual orientation IT wishes to pursue … it might change tomorrow, but we have to accept this as a reality and a normality for others, and for ourselves. How does a society like this comprehend what is going on around it? When we conclude that logic is a matter of opinion, then all the rules you can think of do not apply!

It is a free for all, and no one is running the bus, and the bus will soon run out of road, if not fueled before then. This madness is not unusual since it happened in the '20s, '50s, and later on in the '70s. As Freemasons, we look at these ideologies as a science. We are fascinated not by the media, who stumbles from one story to the next, but by the story itself, and how it will affect others. If we are not careful with our past, and we let our imagination carry us away, we will make big mistakes with our society. What we think technology has brought us is a misconception. We actually brought technology; we invented technology. Long ago, when there was no square, ruler, or method of finding where north and south, east and west were located, our society knew where those locations were because we gave these locations a name. We named everything on this planet, and we continue to do so. We are creatures of creation who are capable of creating others like us. But we still do not accept this gift. We tend to consider it nothing more than a technique, and it is not a technique; it is imbedded in all humanity for the best, most solitary purposes.

We made all of the races, and we gave all of the races on this planet a name and a title. Most importantly, we even gave those races of people a position in life, and those positions are held by force of the WILL of tyrants and despots—be they sectarian or non-sectarian, ideological or philosophical; it is the WILL of tyrants that has lead us here to the present time. However, nature being what nature is, we have also had well-enlightened men and woman who have come through the ages with ideas, belief systems, and methods for us to become better at what we are … "ARCHITECTS."

We are the architects of this world, but we are not the great artificer of this universe we live in. If we do not come to grips with this, we will never achieve our goals, and in the end, we will destroy ourselves just as other civilizations who came before us have. If we are made of the same materials as the stuff that is found in the stars and the heavens, then we are just another manifestation of creation here on earth. There were other civilizations and other ideas, many of which came and went, each of them adding one more course of bricks onto the temple we are all trying to build in our minds, but nothing will be finished until all are finished … are we getting close to finishing?

Cause and Effect

Is everything truly connected? Are we all part of one big plan? Who makes the decisions and how do they affect all of us? Below is a list of think tanks that exist today. Most of them were developed during or soon after the second world war: (It should be noted here that even today new ones are created. An example is the George Soros organizations exerting influence in many locations around the world. The interesting pattern is the original funding by a wealthy patron grew to a small group of patrons and rapidly to paid professional staff people. As founders pass from the scene, they take on a life of their own, often recruiting business, academic and military leaders and retirees. The propagate thru grants and "research" funding. And virtually all of them lobby national governments.)

The Center for Strategic and International Studies (CSIS) is a Washington, D.C. think tank. It was founded in 1962 by Admiral Arleigh Burke and David Ab-shire "at the height of the Cold War, dedicated to the simple but urgent goal of finding ways for America to survive as a nation and prosper as a people." Today, "CSIS experts conduct research and analysis and develop policy initiatives" on issues related to U.S. defense policy and international security, "global challenges" such as "population, energy security, global health, technology, and the international financial and economic system," and regional studies.

The Brookings Institution is a century-old American research group on Think Tank Row in Washington, D.C. It conducts research and education in the social sciences—primarily in economics, metropolitan policy, governance, foreign policy, and global economy and development. It's stated mission is to "provide innovative and practical recommendations that advance three broad goals: strengthen American democracy; foster the economic and social welfare, security and opportunity of all Americans; and secure a more open, safe, prosperous, and cooperative international system."

The Cato Institute is an American Libertarían think tank headquartered in Washington, D.C. It was founded as the Charles Koch Foundation in 1974 by Ed Crane, Murray Rothbard, and Charles Koch, chairman of the board and chief executive officer of the conglomerate Koch Industries. In July 1976, the name was changed to the Cato Institute. Cato was established to have a focus on public advocacy, media exposure and societal influence. According to the 2014 Global Go To Think Tank Index Report (Think Tanks and Civil Societies Program, University of Pennsylvania), Cato is number 16 in the "Top Think Tanks Worldwide" and number 8 in the "Top Think Tanks in the United States." Cato also topped the 2014 list of the budget-adjusted ranking of international development think tanks.

The Center for American Progress (CAP) is a progressive public policy research and advocacy organization. According to CAP, the center is "dedicated to improving the lives of all Americans, through bold, progressive ideas, as well as strong leadership and concerted action." The Center presents a liberal viewpoint on economic and social issues. It has its headquarters in Washington, D.C.

There are a number of these think tanks in the U.S. Most of them are headquartered in Washington D.C., and all of them do very similar inquiries on how, why, when, and where society is heading. Considering the number of years these organizations have been around and taking into account the numerous issues we have experienced throughout the century, one can only speculate as to what in fact is the true agenda of these organizations. With countless resources—not to mention influential individuals—it would strike me as an impossibility that what we are experiencing today is by chance. It becomes a gambler's dream when those in power refuse to accept the outcomes of these ideas that are developed in these think tanks. But one thing is for sure: if you are not on their watch list, you basically don't exist.

To this list you can also add the numerous other organizations that do not necessarily function as a think tank but rather a watch dog: human rights organizations, labor unions, religious institutions with their own set of watch dogs, and let's not forget the media think tanks who provide the masses with a predigested feast and a pharmacy to go along with it in case your stomach is upset after you hear the news. Sound familiar? Excluding technology, same pattern repeated for millennia.

It is quite impossible to leave out some simple facts about the think tanks of today, and the think tanks of the past. Long ago, when FM∴ was a leading think tank in Europe, Latin America, and later in the U.S., there was a sort of moral compass, and that moral compass was simply handed down from one lodge to another. You would think that if this Moral Compass were still in existence that we today would be a more civilized world—no hunger, no slavery, no wars … The results are quite the opposite; in fact, nothing has changed. And this is not because FM∴ failed to do its job, it isn't because modern think tanks can't do their job, it's not even because we do not posses the technology to rid ourselves of these ailments that we carry with us form one century into another. It is simply because we no longer understand what it means to be human and in harmony with one another.

This Humanist understanding is taught through degrees in FM∴—the keepers of the royal secret. Which is not a big secret at all; it's actually more mathematical than it is philosophical. It's called "harmony." We are no longer in tune with the universal music of harmony—to live in harmony with one another. Free Masons look forward to meeting, because it brings harmony in their life. This universal harmony has been expressed throughout the ages, and even though FM∴ has been demonized by many, criticized by the ignorant, and challenged by the fools who claim to know it, Free Masonry has survived it all.

But to what sacrifice? What have we sacrificed in order to survive the ages? This answer will probably remain unsolved for now, at least by this writer who looks at it from the outside looking inward. And perhaps this is our duty—to look inward in order to understand our own faults, flaws, and weaknesses in order to help ourselves, so that we can in tern help others.

In order to understand the construct of FM∴, we have to understand the true purpose for its formation. FM∴ was founded during a time of persecution, both by church and state—a time where the opinion of the intellectual was monitored and censored. To have a group or organization that was not controlled by church or government (or king) was unheard of and illegal. So FM∴ enlisted the membership of some of those individuals; thus, assuring themselves of certain rights and privileges. But the fundamental purpose was to express freely amongst a group of like-minded individuals, ideas, plans, and designs that would change the way the nations functioned. It worked marvelously for several centuries; however, when FM∴ enlisted the membership of individuals who served two masters, FM∴ began to fail.

As a think tank, FM∴ basically drifted aside and became something more like a men's club that practices ritual rites of passage, memorizes lectures, awards itself metals and jewels, but represents nothing in society. With less than 3 million members in the U.S., FM∴ is by no means a power house of an organization. Free Masonry does not solicit funds from members or non-members through the sales of books, magazines, etc. Most of our lodges are dilapidating due to lack of funds for repair, as well as due to low membership. Lodges survive through the dues payments that are sent out once a year. As fund managers, they are very good at it. What Free Masons mostly do today is support charities, sponsor hospitals (like the Shriners Hospital), and many other charitable organizations. It is said that Free Masons donate over a million dollars a day to charitable organizations. Whether that is true or not, I would not know, since I have never managed such departments. But with so many appendant bodies, there is a very high probability that the donations are in fact in the millions of dollars. In a book published during the 18th century called *Pythian Knighthood*, the writer comments that during the 18th century, the Masons, Odd Fellows, and the Pythians, had donated in excess of 2 million dollars to charitable organizations.

The Free Masons, the Odd Fellows, and the Pythians sponsored, financed, fed, and housed thousands of orphans all over the United States, not to mention the halfway houses and housing for abused woman and children. It was not until the middle of the 19th century that you see most of these operations going toward government funding and government management. It was not because the Masons, Odd Fellows, and Pythians were not doing a good job, it was because these institutions were losing members much faster than they could bring them in, and with no members, you had no funding to keep these charities operational. The public lost interest in these organizations; after all, who the heck wants to be a moralist.

To sum up these few chapters, we have looked at what FM∴ was, is, and has become. We see that our decisions today are not necessarily devised by the *will* of the people, but rather by the influence of some important people in some important positions—mainly think tanks. The expanse of the think tanks of today is far reaching, and to think that everything is by chance is not only foolish but stupid at best. The connection of these think tanks with other smaller perhaps less intrusive or invasive institutions (who are also able to make changes in society—perhaps not as impactful or permanent, but persistent and well capable to say the least) is more than obvious in our society today.

We have also learned that we are connected as a race of humans on a small planet, and that the connections we have are in fact mystical at best. Since the complete science of the mind is not yet available, we are left with many mysteries. But one thing is for certain, whatever you can think of, others will do the same, even if they never had any contact with you or your ideas. It was once thought that Leonardo De Vinci was a great inventor and that he had developed flying machines as well as tanks and underwater diving apparatus; however, this was far from the truth. The truth is, and was, and will forever be that Leonardo was a talented man whose methods of painting is still to this day a mystery, but his inventions were not his; they were the ideas of others who came before him but were close to him, and Leonardo simply added some perfection or improvements to the designs of others.

And the sad thing is that Leonardo never took credit for designing them. It has been the historians who have mistakenly awarded this genius something he did not ask for—or perhaps it was not a mistake at all, but simply the work of a few Europeans who wanted to make a point: did everything of talent came from Europe during the age of enlightenment? If everything we know of history is not as it seems, is it possible that history itself is not correct?

The Science of Media and Journalism

Should we, after what we have discussed and learned on our own, trust what the media, or the journalists tell us? Is there still journalism out there? When we look at the news media, we normally see a few individuals who hire what they call "experts." Sometimes these experts are former FBI, CIA, NSA, and retired judges, lawyers, people that should influence your decision on a matter that may or may not impact your livelihood.

Sometimes the news seems more like a pharmacy where you can find a remedy for whatever ails you, and sometimes the news media can be a sickness. How many times can you stand to watch injustice committed upon one race of people? How many times can you stand to watch death and ignorance as they are portrayed by the news media? Who is the media trying to convince? One week everything is falling apart, and the next week everything is doing so well that our plates are overflowing. If I were trying to put a psychological status on the news media, I would say that it suffers from some sort of bipolar disorder with a severe case of paranoia. Today, every news channel is trying to conquer the *truth meter*. Every news media claims that they are honest, trustworthy, and offer-up-to-the-minute news on what is happening around the world. Can't we do this ourselves? There is such a thing as the internet, and there are chat rooms to where you can go and find out not only what the weather is like in China, but also talk with a Chinese person and have them give you a real view of what it's like to live there. There is also the millions of books written by authors who have not only experienced everything the news media claims to have skilled resource for, but you also can pick what side the story is coming from. Not everything is black and white, true or false; there are gray areas wherein we do not know exactly what the issues are.

We live in a world of illusions, and at best these illusions carry us into the future—sometimes without us even knowing. The problem is when countries do not share the same illusions as ours, or we do not share the same illusions as they. The lack of harmony, the simple act of not respecting one's privacy and acknowledging each other's purpose in life is the catalyst for why we lack harmony with one another. It is speculated that one of the many reasons for the news media attacking—or rather showing—what the police and policing of the people is doing, as far as its state of corruption and immorality, is simply because they're looking for another method of policing the masses. This will also bring a change in the manner in which we judge the public; hence, the courtroom, the court system, and the correctional institution is also about to change. ("Confide in me the secrets of society and death, so that I may better understand it, so that I may better understand my own departure.")

FM∴ as a science studies these events and many others, but it would not be correct to say that each and every Free Mason out there is doing this, nor would it be correct to say that this is what Free Masonry is about today. But for some of the members of this institution, these topics are of interest because they bring us back in focus with what is going on around us. You cannot live like sheep; governments are not religious leaders; they do not tend to a flock. They simply guide the flock (or the pubic) in a direction that they (the governments of the world) believe to be the right path, but it is the will of the people to decide what that path will ultimately be If they have the will and under the most severe conditions, as in the past, if they are willing to pay the price for the exercise of their will.

We have seen in the past decade a number of changes in our constitution, we have seen presidents gain unprecedented power over the public, and we have seen abuse in the court system, the policing system, and the correctional institutions. None of which has either deterred or prevented individuals from becoming victims of abuse. The number of institutions today who inform us on the illegitimacy of our government are few and far between. For the most part, you have single individuals making these calls, and most of the time, those said individuals are scrutinized if not demonized by the media, government, and other institutions. Conspiracy theories have run away with the public; today, everything is a conspiracy that will never be solved, and still we wait for that knight in shining armor to come by and rescue our ideals, our thoughts, our integrity—but the knights of long ago are no longer. And chivalry is not what armies fight for anymore. It's time to stop and think about our next step, and as today tensions grow with North Korea, we wonder who will pose the next challenge. Hopefully, our next challenge should be keeping harmony with one another. And so, the challenge before us as a Fraternity is to find and keep the core of our values as the light to which we allegorically elude not only for the sake of our Fraternity, but for the sake of mankind.

CHAPTER 3

Speculative Masonry

With speculative masonry we learn to act upon the square and maintain secrecy. This part is also interwoven with religions because it is the part of masonry that does not deal with architecture, form, or structure of the physical sort, but rather the esoteric, mystical, and spiritual side of man. Here, I will attempt to explain the age-old mystery of what the power of god on earth is, and how man wields that power.

All civilizations left their mark on earth through architecture. It is from here that we even bother to study long lost societies because it is what will first be seen perturbing from the ground. Long before we can see skeletons, clothing, or remnants of a civilization, we will see its edifices as they stretch their arms to call upon those of us who have forgotten them all together.

Most if not all civilizations destroyed the history of others in order to create their own history. All conquerors, from the Persians to the Greeks, destroyed anything that was evidence of technology, medicine, and science and replaced it as their own in order to make their history the one and only. This also went along with religious beliefs as well as philosophical principles written in their belief system ... whatever they may be.

Before Christianity, back when there were thousands of pagan belief systems, most if not all pagan religions fought for territory on a small scale. These pagan belief systems had little influence over the territorial control of the many people who wandered for thousands of miles through landscapes that were unknown to those wonderers. How far *man* ventured in quest for survival—*not* God or gods— is unknown. However, the evidence unearthed by many scholars today paint a different picture of the history we read in school. Christianity is a creation of man, not of god. So too are the rest of the world's religions; they are a creation of the creature called "man"— not God. God has one universal belief system, and it is either acceptable, palatable, or recognizable only by the creature called man. No other life from on the planet acknowledges, bows down to, or gives homage to God other than man: the creature of intelligence created by Him: the Great Architect— Builder of all—It that was and forever shall be—the one who presented itself to Moses and said, "I will be what I will be has sent you." "I will be what I will be," not "I am that I am." There is a difference between the two expressions. One came first, and it was later changed for reasons that are unknown because it would have been the first time in any historical book, such as the Bible, that an entity with no name presented itself in the first person: "I am that I am."

Whoever wrote this story, be it Moses or whoever, the concept of speaking about yourself in the first person is an acknowledgment of the *will* of a creator— not a creature. Something spoke to Moses, and I will not enter upon a discussion of religious beliefs only about the incident. Moses was hearing something and visualizing something before his eyes, and it spoke to him in a language that he under- stood. Or did Moses stand and meditate on a mirage? An Egyptian trained by priest, now turned outcast Jew, he came to the realization of who, and what, he and everyone else was. Regardless of how less sensational that may have been, many events in history are less sensational than what was written by historians.

Moses was an architect. A builder and a priest, he left all that he had to find silence, and in doing so, he found the essence of the Creator God in an event on top of a mountain. So gifted was Moses that this event took place more than once, and he marveled at the results as others marveled at his *will* to bring a people together and also to end a struggle that had long been predicted by his own race of people. If there was no Moses, there would have been no Jewish people. Moses put the Jews back on the map and back on the course they had started hundreds of years prior. We cannot prove any of this scientifically; archeologists will argue the very existence of Moses himself—never mind the Exodus. Historians will argue as to when the Exodus, the Old Kingdom, the Middle Kingdom, and the New Kingdom of Egypt could have occurred, but they will not claim the Exodus as a fact. They are unable to make a distinction between any race of people that may cause conflict amongst others who are not named in a Holy book. Religion holds hostage the minds of many, and sometimes as with the many incidents of terror that we still see today, religion encompasses these events and holds them at bay. Revealing information of a race of people who were gifted in thought, architecture, science, and ingenuity will only stir up the emotions of others who, for some reason known only to the Great Creator, do not possess such talents, can, will, and have caused violence of all types.

We in America today are going through one of the most dramatic—if not social-egotistic, self-centered, and capricious—rants that any civilization will experience. Americans today are rediscovering their child tantrum experiences. They want it now, and they want it all—instant gratification with no regard for the outcome of the events. Sad.

We are destroying monuments today as barbaric civilizations and advanced civilizations have done in the past. We have in essence learned nothing of the Creator, and we have let the creature become the god or gods. In the following pages I will explain why man, the creature, decided to be God, the creator. Obsessed with power, the greed for attention and reverence, and the lust of worldly things, man became god. No longer did

God speak to his creatures on hill tops, for his creatures' army leveled every single hill. The creature, man, made the earth bow her mountain tops to him (or at least the creature feels that the mountains have been conquered by the advent of flight). But Masons know better, or they should.

The Templar knights did find something while digging around in Israel and the temple. They found a system of mathematics that is known as *sacred mathematics*. It is architectural mathematics that enables builders to fabricate with sacred geometry—that which gives a structure made of cold stones the presence or essence of the great Creator God. This is the source of God's power on earth, not by the ordinance of the Creator, but by the imagination of its creature, man. There are no magic dishes, no box with holy relics, just a blueprint of how to build any or all of the above. How you build these relics is dependent upon the mindset of the creature, man, at the time. During the conquest, reconquest, or crusader event, what was sought after by the Christian Church leaders was the *sacred geometry* that made these large edifices of worship possible. And if you cannot accept that, consider that the crusaders were in fact architects, builders, themselves.

After the 12th century, you begin to see the Muslim style of architecture used all over Europe. Not even the Greeks were as ornate as the Persian architects—not by a long shot. The ratio of 1/3 was used in all of the temple buildings built by the Muslim invaders and their architects. The style by which they created depth with the use of continuous arches was done previously by the Egyptians with columns, but nothing says it better than an arch. Whereas an arch is an entryway, a column is but a support, and in many cases a stumbling block around which you have to go in order to pass. Columns were representations of establishments, but arches are a door to the kingdom of heaven here on earth. What the Christian Church did is just that: they build the kingdom of heaven here on earth—temporary, but a kingdom nonetheless. While other civilizations grew with lavish structures, the Christian Church grew with structure, form, and of course a temporary kingdom ... until the real one comes.

When the Christian Knights saw these magnificent structures, such as the one in Cordoba Spain, it was obvious to them that they had stumbled across what would bring God into the European churches later built everywhere in Europe. The

Moors were adamant about writing down ideas and designs, unlike the Greeks and the Egyptians who, for the most part, did not work off a drawing. It is known that the knowledge of sacred geometry did not come from the Christian European, but rather the Muslim with who they were at war. And the Church did a great deal of burying information, but what was important for the Knights and the Church was the geometry that would inspire the Christian faith and in essence bring God into the Christian temples.

The idea of institutions formed by the Crusades (all Christian military orders) was what gave the European countries (dominated by the Moors) a reason to side with the Christian faith. The Christian faith offered so many institutions, and none of this would have been possible if it were not for those noble men who took up arms against an enemy that kept them and their people form prospering. Those noble men—who were not ruled by Kings or governed by the Church—are the ones that history forgets. They were Architects that governed themselves accordantly with the implementation of institutions that were to further guide and stabilize their re-conquest of these nations, which were taken over by the Moors. And it is because these noble men that we have such a vast and endless metaphysical system that continues to this day. If it were not for the Crusades, there would have never been the ideas seen in the many institutions we have today—none. There is no exception to the rule. The Crusade—and I will reiterate what I feel must be said more than once—crated Europe through a system of institutions, organizations, lodges, facilities, and establishments that are still around and are still being used today.

Since we are discussing speculative Masonry, we must try to understand that what happened in the past cannot be hidden from the present. The establishment of institutions went hand in hand with the developing of a country. Mathematical models and the think tanks of today were no different than the think tanks of the past; mathematics is as old as time itself. However, what we have to accept as human beings is that not all institutions, organizations, or establishments are for the greater good of *all* mankind. The Moors had institutions, architects, mathematicians, schools, hospitals, and a form of taxation to keep all of this working. What they did not have is the notion that, out of nowhere and for no reason, an individual may rise up, and either debunk, refute, or outright disregard the institutions, educational systems, and hospitality of said type of government. Even today we see that institutions impose their will on the people. The institution wavered with time, and many if not all institutions became an entity on their own—a sort of crusader type organization whose malevolent ideology is at best described as diabolical. As society grew, these institutions grew ahead of them, and they are governed by regulations from all sides; government and religious influences are abundant.

Our court rooms today, which at best can be described as a casino, are probably one of the fastest growing institutions everywhere on the planet. Court rooms were a modern invention, found necessary in order for those who disagreed with establishments to have some type of equal respect under a variety of laws. Today, with the formation of electronically dependent and socially isolated citizens, the fast access to information, and the ability to turn everything into anyone's favor, the court rooms of are at best antiquated yet still effective.

When I say that the modern court rooms are effective, I do not mean that they are honest, trustworthy, or that they represent truth and justice for all. This may be possible, but perhaps in a small town where the population is less than a thousand, and more than likely those townspeople would have to travel to a bigger city in order to settle legal disputes. Our court system is at best described as a centers of special interest negotiations and suppressors of those who mat wittingly or unwittingly offend one of them. run by different conglomerates. Think tanks offer mathematical models to ensure a 95% success rate on many of the cases tried by the government, and government housing (i.e. the prison system) helps out by providing the guilty and the innocent with virtually inhuman warehousing for whatever time they are sentenced. The correctional institutions of this nation, and all others with exception given only to Sweden, are in fact a destitute place for anyone to be in, especially if you are innocent. And unfortunately, many thousands who are incarcerated in our American prisons are innocent, but the mathematical models used by the prosecution and the courts today allow for a totalitarian judicial system to exist, free from any accountability.

There are virtually no indictments or arrest charges that lead to lengthy prison time for prosecutors and judges as well as courts who use these facilities and institutions as a means to enforce tyranny on the individuals who cross paths with the law. And the courts continue with no oversight, no evaluation, and no penalty for errors committed by their part. None. Who can prosecute the king if the king owns all the courts, justices, and attorneys? Who can prosecute the tyrant if the tyrant owns the land, the governments, the courts, and everything in between? Did the Crusades actually save us, or did they actually create a system of checks and balances that only exist if you're at the top? Would the wrong actually admit to being wrong? Is it possible that our system believes that everyone is guilty until proven innocent?

And some say that this is a big advantage to how things were in the middle ages. Yes, it is, but this is why the crusades occurred. This is why revolutions are started. Typical scenario: you use a friend's car, and your friend left his drug prescription in the car. You are stopped by the police for a minor traffic infraction, the police officer sees the drugs, and since you can prove that your name is not on the prescription and you can prove that the drugs are not yours, you're safe, but only after you are arrested for possession, went to court, and spent several thousand dollars on something you did not do. Then you are back on the street with a record that if you do not pay to get it removed, you will probably never be able to find a decent job ever again. That is really all it takes for your freedom and your privileges to be taken away from you.

Does it happen—sure it does. And the criminal justice system is profoundly unresponsive even when it is clear that evidence was withheld, new evidence uncovered, innocence clearly established, and the wrongfully convicted person languishes in prison for years. Any internet search on this will reveal tragically large numbers of cases of it and organizations, many comprising law school students, struggling with a problem never contemplated by the members off our Fraternity who founded our Country. And our Fraternity actually teaches us to not sit back silently, yet we do.

Nor is the Justice System unique in the domination by institutional forces contradictory to the teachings of our Fraternity. Think through the esteemed interests related to homelessness. It is a major industry and the victims are seldom helped in any major way except by the human compassion shown by individuals.

"Nothing said is nothing heard"

We are going to go through various institutions in the coming years, where we will find small control groups with interests pursuant to Think Tank cults within them that seem to be the dominating factor in the continuation of its methodology. Many times, in the past, these institutions developed through a fanaticism of sorts. If we look at why the Crusades began in the East, we see that a surge in patriotism and religious inspiration moved thousands toward a land which many called the Holy Land, but if the Holy were around to advise them, they would have said God is everywhere not just in the Holy Land, then the crusades would have probably never taken place. Even though the crusades were 400 years too late, what started the crusades was not an evangelical movement, but rather the patriotism of those who felt oppressed by another group who had long since tired society out with their kidnappings and enslavement of Christians. The Saracens are not to be confused with the Muslims; the Turks came first, then the Moors, and with them came the Muslim religion that had been slowly growing in the East. Naked and poor, these men were inspired by Mohammed who led them through battles that at best served as inspiration or miracles from God that their newfound profit, Mohammad, was going to lead them to take over the world. The faith of the Mohammedans has been described as a religion of dominion and war. This was no different a feeling than that which the early crusaders felt when they ventured to the East in an attempt to conquer the Holy Land. However, the Crusades' venture formed most of Europe, and the Saracens for the most part were scattered into every corner of the world. Nonetheless, these are very large institutions, and by studying them we see where society may fail.

When the world was being ravaged by Goths, Huns, and vandals, pilgrimages never ceased because the pilgrims were never really bothered by the threats, and in many cases, the would-be assailants looked at these early Christian pilgrims as harmless in their quest. The assailants knew that with these pilgrimages would come a force to protect the Christians. God is everywhere, not just in Jerusalem. The Pilgrimages had become more important than the faith itself.

Here we have something to learn about many of the institutions of today— where they are interested more in the trip than they are the purpose of the institution for the long term. It took several hundred years for the early and late church fathers to figure this out, and it was also not even considered by the rulers until much later in history that institutions played an important role in the development of a society. But to what extent do these institutions play a role in the psychological development of a society? There is where our problem lies. Our society is suffering a serious psychological meltdown, and for the most part, it has transferred to our ruling class and is making its way through each and every institution in the world. This psychological problem is a world problem.

Our Fraternity occurred, grew and developed in the presence of cycles of control and overreach by small groups of controlling interests and the battles for freedom of action and freedom of thought. We are taught today to be peaceful citizens obedient to the laws under which we live—yet were created to combat injustice and tyranny of thought and action. One look at the Cuban Revolution and our role in it shows us just how far American Masonry strayed from what the Fraternity actually teaches us in only one century.

We have men who are discharged from our own military, who are now in the present-day volunteer fighters in a war against the same enemy the crusaders fought over a thousand years ago. What does that tell us about the many institutions that the crusaders set up back in the 12th and 13th century, and all throughout the rest of European history? What does Freemasonry teach us about this?

Here is a bigger and more important question—what in essence is really catastrophic is the psychological meltdown of an institution that has failed in every way to instill and to continue to instill an idea that is not dead but simply has been used as a tool to insight the masses into a conflict that could have been avoided altogether. History repeats itself and we have learned nothing. Is it because the moral and ethical fabric of society once engineered by Freemasonry by our Founding Fathers has been lost to all but a few of us? The answer is obviously yes. And so, what do we do about it?

Again, "where are the think tanks?" Where are the brain boxes of the 1940s when you need them? Why have those systems failed us as well? Again and again we revert back to the Crusades and the formation of Europe. As the plot thickens, so too does the understanding of the construct of Freemasonry. The Crusades were done not only to preserve what the newfound religion, Christianity, had made and brought to the Western world, it also wanted the relics back. Somehow the illustrious families of Rome at the time of the early state of the crusades came to seek refuge or asylum in Jerusalem, and on the tomb of Jesus the Christ, these early Christians found on the banks of the river Jordan what seemed to be missing or vanquished form the rest of the world.

In other words, the royal society or the really wealthy found that wealth mattered little; what was important was peace and harmony, and that peace and harmony was missing everywhere in the world ... or so it seemed to these illustrious families. The armies of Khosrow, king of Persia, took the relics of the Church of the Christ and robbed it of all its religious artifacts, including the cross of the Savior Jesus the Christ and carried it off. It took 10 years before Heraclius, after many reverses, triumphed, brought back to Jerusalem the many Christians whose chains of bondage he had broken, and carried with him as he entered the city the true cross of Jesus on his shoulders. The victory of the Christians was short lived, however. During the beginning of the seventh century there had arisen, in an obscure corner of Asia, a new religion. It opposed all other religions and preached dominion and war. Mohammed had promised his disciples that he would conquer the world with this new-found faith, and he lead a crusade of Arabs, whom he persuaded with miracles and triumph in the battlefield. This new faith and its miracles and success increased the confidence of his partisans; it carried conviction to the minds of the weak and wavering. After the death of the prophet of Mecca, his lieutenants and followers of his first exploits carried on his great work.

Another prophet with another desire to rule the world with his message of conquest and war … sound familiar? The difference with the true followers of Jesus of Nazareth was their lack of interest in human conquest. They were followers of a state of mind. It is much later that we see Christians burning down libraries and persecuting one another. The followers of Mohammed wanted the same thing the Christians and the Jews had. Everyone wanted a piece of Jerusalem and the Church of the Holy Sepulcher as if this place possessed some secret power that made the world turn. It has been so much so, that it is still the stuff of legends. There are mysteries that surround Jerusalem, the temple of Solomon, and the many artifacts that Christians, Jews, and Muslim alike have killed for, or died to keep, relish, and worship as trinkets that we can either touch or wear around our necks.

The meaning of the psychological dysfunction of society is a far cry from the many events that took place and the many institutions that were established to keep these psychological dysfunctions at bay well into the 16th century. The pilgrims and the shrines became the center focus for this Christian religion that had developed for over 700 years since the death of Jesus the Christ and the many churches that were erected to him. Followers flocked to Jerusalem to see the proof that had been concealed from them. This was a time where followers ventured to places that were hostile, dangerous, and many lost their lives in doing so. But this drive—whether you call it faith, patriotism, or just the passion that we as humans all possess—is what leads us to where we are now.

And now we begin to see the where and how of the meaning of Freemasonry relates to each of us today.

To understand the underlying problem of the many institutions that were established prior to or soon after the Crusades, which basically created Europe, would take several volumes of books, perhaps even an entire library to explain. And who has the time to do this? We today receive messages via email, newspapers (for those who still read them), and the Television (with its many experts, views, opinions, and will to make things go the way they want them to go). I was not around during the Crusades and neither was anyone alive today, but many of us have been above ground long enough to have seen the newscasts of the '60s, '70s, and '80s, and we do remember that television news never had experts on the show to give us their opinion on matters that we relied on from the institutions that were already in existence. Were some of these institutions replaced or did we as a people simply stop believing in the institutions of the past and relied mostly on instant news? Experts are called by the television media news to give the pubic some sort of reassurance that the press was looking out for their well-being, and today with cell phone technology (that we cannot seem to live without) and computers that can run a house while you are away from home, our desire to further psychologically examine ourselves as human beings has caused us to further remove ourselves from the reality that has been with us since the beginning.

The reality is that we are here on our own; nothing and nobody is coming to help us unless we evoke that help from our own consciousness. Consciousness is that which every prophet who practiced harmony and peace preached. The lack of *harmony* has been the fall of all society since the beginning of time because we seek what we cannot have at an instance or at a moment's notice. (After going through hurricane Irma without electricity or utility services for 8 days—no television, no radio, just "work" to keep the family fed, clean, and comfortable—one can easily see that what we live for is one another, and that is the end of it.)

This we know and it is at the heart of our Fraternity, Religion instills virtues in a society; it gives hope to those who are tired and weak, but none of this is possible without the harmony that is within each and every human being on the planet. A cross raised high upon a hill with no one to see or worship it is nothing more than a tree growing on a hill top until it reaches the sky or falls to the ground. The many monuments we have built are for us as creatures of God to wonder about; the relics of the past are there for us to think on. However, the institutions of which number in the U.S. up to 1,500 and the think tanks have failed to produce harmony within our societies, and on a global scale they have left millions of homes half-built.

We are indeed great builders, but we are poor contractors since we never really want to find a way to finish what we were created to do in the first place: establish peace and harmony with one another in order to make this small planet of ours a more hospitable and harmonic place in which to live. Our ability to subdue our passions and keep our desires within due bounds amongst all our neighbors, especially our own flesh and blood, has been a magnanimous task, and this task is one that no multitude of institutions or think tanks can fix.

Imagine if today we could all go out and look at the sky at night and behold the beauty of the heavens, the firmament below which we stand, and ask ourselves do we really wish to continue on this path of war and desolation or do we really want to make this world our home, because this is the decision that we have to make today—the decision which we should have made one hundred years ago. Today with technology we can make it happen, or we can simply destroy ourselves and leave nothing but a few monuments for the earth to swallow up or wash away. Nature has her way in the end. This earth will rid herself of us and everything, as it has done in the past. As the Nazarene once said, "the kingdom of God is in front of your very nose, and you do not see it. If you cannot see the visible, how then can you see the invisible?

Armed with whatever individual resources we may have and understanding what our Fraternity teaches us together with a faith in those teachings, we live an evolving socialism that will in the end be an example of what apparently invisible hands would like society to be. Our media today is leading society by way of sensationalism, and in doing so, will exercise changes that make us lead our society and the rest of the world—Europe leading the way—to an exemplification of socialism as it was never imagined to be. We may well find ourselves working basically for nothing, and there are about 50 million in the U.S. that do not work or have worked very little. Socialism teaches that this is acceptable; since everything today comes from perhaps a handful of distributors, manufacturers, and dealers, it's not very difficult to understand how easy it would be to convince society to simply work and go and get whatever they want. The idea of the distribution of wealth as president Obama once said is not as farfetched as many would presume to believe. Those that like to work will likely continue to do so, and those that don't will be accommodated; it's really that simple and expected.

We are led to believe this utopian process will lead to a better society, yet it is not what the think tanks of today are working on. The lack of interest in self-reliance or self-sacrifice has taken on a different definition—one that today is on an extremely individual basis. When you see the wealth of a nation or the wealthy in a nation give away their property and their money, you can say with all certainty that everything is now integrated into one system—not one person or entity, but a system where true wealth is the knowledge of all things, not a piece of paper that is backed by nothing other than an absurd idea of shimmering stones that once entranced the eyes of the ancients. Yet even they understood that you cannot either eat or nourish yourself with gold or precious stones. It has been the ignorant that lead even the wealthy to be tyrants.

No illness can survive without a host, and as many illnesses that exist today, ignorance appears to arise without reason. It is as if we summoned ignorance to take over so we can hope that knowledge will come to the rescue and continue the emotional and sensational lifestyle. This is the way of ignorance; it brought about the inquisition, wars, famine, and continues to do the same to this very day. The hope is that this "ignorance" will not last very long. The clock is ticking, and soon we will face the reality of a socialism unlike any other, but so long as it is in harmony with what society wants, it will work … At least for some time, until there is another change. The question is, will that peace and harmony be achieved by us or be imposed on us. And so, as Masons we each face the profound decision as to when and how to act, if at all. The answer to that lies in what we are taught, and there are brothers about you, if you can find them, who may be able to help you face the question. The answer, however, is yours and yours alone.

I look forward to our meetings at some of these appendant bodies. This is not because there is much of an intellectual discussion, but because it teaches me something about human nature. I can sometimes picture many of the syndicates or institutions of the past as they slowly began to become less and less influential. The membership probably dwindled with the years and the decades that followed. But the mindset of those coming in is not like that of those of the past. Hence, you have an institution, or a syndicate, but it runs more like a museum and like not a fully functioning organization.

None of this offends me; it, in fact, educates me on something about the past. Did the Templar knight really get the short end of the stick? or did the ruling bodies of the Templar knights simply give up because they had lost most of the intellectual leadership needed to carry these institutions or syndicates to further heights?

Belonging to several of the largest charitable fraternities in the United States, I can with confidence say that the knowledgeable individuals that could have made something out of these syndicates are in fact nowhere to be found. Perhaps we lost many of them due to wars, disease, and old age. And since there are fewer and fewer of these individuals to go around, we see what we see.

This is also a reflection of our current and past Washington administration. It has, apparently seen the last of the intellectual free thinkers. What is left are individuals giving themselves the presidency, the senate seat, the congress seat, and even the highest seat of all: the priesthood. It goes without saying, "Man must be ruled by God or he shall be governed by tyrants." I say man must govern himself or he and she will be governed by idiots.

The beauty of institutions is or ought to be what they help with, and even though most if not all of these institutions are incongruent with one another, the basis for their formation can still be found; you only need the desire to look for them. The institutions of today, as those of yesteryear, serve as the government of the people. The people are the government the extent that they either impose their collective will or suffer the result of passive acceptance, and the government consists of the public and its 1,500 institutions that help make the city, town, and state work in a synchronized manner—all of it going to one central place: Washington D.C., where those whom we elect to be our spokespersons for our views, our ideas, and our integrity, are elected to a position where they are our connection to the thousands of institutions that make up our system of government. The world is much more complicated than it looks, and our system of leadership is much more complex than that of any other nation. But our system is as old as the formation of Europe, and it continues to follow the network of syndicates used in Europe in the "re-conquest." Our biggest problem is that our institutions have become dysfunctional, and a dysfunctional family cannot by any means teach or educate a functional family, nor can *disorder* comprehend *order*.

The failure of our institutions to comprehend the very nature of respect, harmony, and care for the well-being both mentally and physically of its own people is why we are living in a nation with many rooms, and everyone is keeping away from each other. Contact, discussions of disclosure, and the argument of intellect (not intellectual argument) are nowhere to be found. Our Fraternity teaches, in fact compels, us to address this although its leadership today is as adrift as the rest of our leadership. We have three court rooms: one for the poor, one for the wealthy, and one for those who are above the law. The courts for the poor are filled with white color crimes, of which its criminals have never committed any crime prior to their convictions—the system used by prosecutors in which one person is rewarded for snitching on another; whether or not the crimes are related makes no difference. The excessive sentences, the cover ups, the fabricated stories used by prosecutors, and the many judges that aid them in their desperate climb of the legal corporate ladder pays very little attention to the damage it has done and is doing to so many woman in the penal system today. In order to clearly understand this monster, you have to get inside of it; you have to visit the detention and correctional facilities of the state of Florida and the dilapidating state of condition that many are in. No one cares that woman all across America under the Obama administration were targeted by this crazed war against medicare crime; there never was medicare crime, just medicare mismanagement by the very people who run it—the government—who makes the loop holes and creates the conditions for failure to occur.

No one robs the government of funds; the government robs itself. It takes it out of one pocket and puts it in the other, and then it calls out, "I've been robbed!"

No revolution happens without a cause; give the public enough discord, hate, and resentment and you will have the perfect recipe for a revolution. Pacifist die on the shores; they never make it to the battlefield, and today the battlefield is in the courts. We have seen how the whole Trump/Russia collusion evolved. We see how easy it is to fabricate and dilute a situation to the advantages of another. What makes anyone think it is any different for them than a sitting president is illogical, but it happens each and every day.

Does our history begin with Rome? Is Greece the only place in the world where intellectual discourse began? Why did the Romans center themselves around Israel? What was in Israel in the first century that by 325, a new/old religion began, and once it took over, it spread all over Europe, the Middle East, Africa, and later in Central and South America? And why do we still argue the question of "Creation and Evolution?" It's been centuries and we are still in the dark about these age-old questions, not because the lack of evidence or research ability, but because we are divided. And yet we as Masons are taught to address open questions with civility and brotherly love—not division.

The will of the people has to be economized—no different than you would contain steam in a pressure tank, and then use that steam or will to move the giant wheels which propel the many thousands of institutions that make up the whole of a nation, if not the world itself. But human steam is driven by fire: the will of the people to "Do!" And without this fire/force, you have nothing—no infrastructure, no coordination between those giving orders and those receiving them—no self-esteem, no honor, and no honesty; thus, causing the giant arms propelled by the steam or will of the people to move the wrong wheels, or gears, and in effect, leading our nation's people away from its focus point. We are nothing but steam, and as we all know, steam is simply absorbed by the atmosphere in nature. Nature needs not the will of the people, nor does it need people to continue its work. We never really tried to understand nature as did the early alchemist who believed that every plant represented a certain part of the body and a cure for that particular part of the human body. They even attributed a planet to the nature of the cure for which a plant was designated to remedy. All this took place in a couple of centuries. The practitioners of the Hermetic arts were burned at the stake, the books written by them confiscated, printing presses were shut down, and the very idea of writing and printing was reserved more as a monitor because we can't read minds—yet. We can, however, read books. The writers of the Hermetic arts were many, and we only see them in chemistry books. They are only mentioned for what they contributed to a particular chapter in the history of science. Avogadro, Paracelsus, Fahrenheit—you read of these individuals in a science book, but not how they came to be or the lives these individuals lived and the era in which they lived. These men were of a Hermetic order, and their practices were conducted in secrecy because failure to do so would lead to certain death, none of which were of natural causes. That wisdom was engendered in the teachings of our Fraternity. Placed in context, it is vital to understanding who we are.

Free Masonry is a science not a religion. It was developed during a time of turmoil and persecution. It has stood as a welcomer of the arts and sciences, and of all philosophical discourse. But our world is changing, and our new generation has become distanced with the cause of creation and has become interested in progress. Technology is good, but progress sometimes is destructive, both mentally and physically. There can be no illness that may last 100 years, nor can there be a body to withstand such an illness. So, in our time, Masons learn, and Masons teach those who wish to learn. And through that process, our Fraternity has survived and will survive— sometimes as only a dim candle, and sometimes as a fiery bush. The difference is each of us.

Carlos De Jesus Verdugo.

POSTSCRIPT

By Ted Connally

It has been a privilege to be a part of the thinking that has gone into this book. The author and I come from somewhat different viewpoints and read some of the source materials through different eyes. Invariably, however, we arrive at the same conclusions and have the same questions.

The ideas and information herein presented should be of interest to and easily understandable by Freemasons as well as students of the periods of history discussed. When printed in Spanish, it will be—in English, perhaps not. Hopefully the book will contribute in some small degree to the reversal in that outcome as it is a sad indictment not only of the Fraternity, but of the remarkable trend of degradation in American education. To its critics I would suggest that there is only what we think we know and what we do not know. To close the chapter on discovery and thought, regardless of the subject, whether by arrogance or ignorance, most assuredly demonstrates the danger and disservice of a closed mind. And there is a lot of that going around these days.

Sunday, January 31, 2021:

as of today there have been hundreds of business, homes, and citizens who have been put in harms way, or have been directly harmed by the countless violent demonstrations by radical groups. For the most part the marxist groups of the Black Lives Matter, and the communist / anarchist groups of ANTIFA (the group our sitting president calls an ideology, not actually a group that exist) have been the leaders in the violent demonstrations and insurrections all across the United States.(All of these violent demonstrations were staged let the truth be known.) More especially in the most liberal of states such as Portland Oregon. A recent peaceful demonstration that went out of control lead by all sides, but mostly nut jobs who believe in Hollywood conspiracy theory such as Q Anon, during a Pro-Trump rally at the capital, lead to the death of three individuals two of which were police officers. (though it is unclear as to what was the actually causation of the deaths of the two officers).

A sitting president who believes in instituting laws without causation, with or without the approval of the House or the Senate. A sitting president who is an insurrectionist, not an abolitionist. A sleeper in the White House who has not a clue as to what comes next or where it will be coming from. An institutional Bomb, who basically has been making money of himself and his family for decades via his positions of power. Joe Biden represents everything that American politics should not be—-corrupt. However corruption is just another part of politics, and as a spider spins its web, so too does Washington politics and the levels of corruption continue to climb, and the higher the tower of Babel is built the greater the level of corruption. Today as DOVO'S, the WHO, the UN, the World Banks and every other conglomerate rate out there plans their next move. The American consortium between these organizations grows more and more involving. Who is finally fools is the sheep, as the wish to know contains not always the faculty to acquire the knowledge, wisdom, and understanding of how they are being used, and for what purpose. Today that an election was ran by braking the constitutional rules, of how elections were run in many states, especially the swing states. Today that machinery that allowed our votes to be sent overseas and then back again to tally up the numbers. Today that we are still uncertain as to who really won an election because both sides refuse to hear, proclaim, or acknowledge the true results, we stand divided once more. It is not unreasonable to say that we are more divided as a nation today in 2021 than we were in 1860, except this has nothing to do with race, creed, nationality, or bigotry, it has though a great deal to do with being able to speak the truth…………..because there is but one truth in this world, and that is, that there is no truth in it! I close with just this one thought; "Unto us a Child is Born, Unto us a Child is Given, and the Government Shall be on His shoulders, and He shall be called Wonderful Councilor, Mighty God, Ever lasting Father, Prince of Peace."Isaiah 9:6-7.

November 5, 2022